Published in the United States of America

ISBN: 978-0-9960741-0-0
Juvenile Fiction / General

This book is
dedicated to my
grandmother,

Catherine.

"Old folks shouldn't be travelin'," said Grandma. "They should stay home where they can be nice and safe."

Grandma sat in her rocking chair in the middle of her living room, rocking back and forth, watching TV like she normally did on any given day.

"Yep, Old folks shouldn't be travelin'."

Grandma's real name was Virginia Loving. She was 92 years old and had lived a very long life. She worked for thirty years selling insurance and had raised two beautiful children, both of whom she loved dearly. During most of those years, she stayed at home where she felt nice and safe.

One day, Grandma realized that she had not seen her grandchildren in a very long time and that made her sad. So she thought, and thought, and thought, and thought, and thought ...

"I want to go and see my grandchildren," Grandma said to Jasmine, one of her favorite grandchildren.

"It's been a long time since I've seen them and I miss them so much."

Jasmine loved her grandma too and would do anything she could to make her happy, so she answered,

"Sure Grandma, but you live in North Carolina and they live in New York. To get there you will have to travel."

"Old folks shouldn't be travelin',"
Grandma said.

Jasmine picked Grandma up the next day from her home in North Carolina. After a few hours they drove through Richmond, Virginia. Jasmine was driving very fast and as they drove, Grandma became unhappy with Jasmine's driving.

Vroom. Vroom.
Vrrrrrrrrrrrrrrrrrrrrrrrrrrrrrrrrrrrroooommm.

"You drive way too fast, Jasmine."

When Jasmine slowed down, she was near the Richmond International Raceway. She had always heard about it, so she drove to the raceway and bought a ticket.

Grandma and Jasmine walked down to the front seats, and just as they sat down, the cars revved their engines. *Vroom. Vroom. Vrrrrrrrrrrrrrrrrrrrrrrrrrrrrrrrrrrrooooommm.* You could tell that the cars were about to go really, really fast; faster than Jasmine. That made Grandma nervous, because she didn't like cars to go too fast. It seemed that when they went fast they also made a lot of noise and smoke.

Grandma looked over the rail and *BOOM!!!* Black smoke covered Grandma's face and made a grumpy grandma mask! *ACHOOOOOOOOOO! Cough! Cough! Cough!* The smoke made Grandma cough and sneeze. A very cranky grandma said, "I should have stayed home. Old folks shouldn't be travelin'."

After they had been driving for a while, Grandma and Jasmine passed the Baltimore Harbor where the Baltimore Aquarium was located and decided to visit.

They wanted to see the many sea creatures, especially the dolphins. Grandma and Jasmine went in to watch the dolphin show, and they decided to sit in the front row.

The show was so much fun. The dolphins were doing all sorts of cool tricks like jumping out of the water and then back in, swirling and splashing each other. When a dolphin did a good job, the trainer gave it a fish.

After performing a summersault in the air, one of the dolphins raced to its trainer for a snack. When the dolphin saw the snack, it was so excited that it spit lots of water out of its mouth. Unfortunately, Grandma was right under the point of the stage where the dolphin was spitting out water. Whiz. Whiz. Whiz. Whiz. Whiz. The water whizzed right onto Grandma. A very wet and sticky Grandma said, "I should have stayed home. Old folks shouldn't be travelin'!"

Jasmine and Grandma then drove up to Ocean City, Maryland where lots of children were playing on the shore. Grandma and Jasmine decided to take a walk and as they walked along the beach, a big gust of wind blew mounds of sand onto Grandma.

Spitting sand out of her mouth Grandma said, "I should have stayed home. Old folks shouldn't be travelin'."

Jasmine and Grandma drove down the Eastern Shore to Assateague Island where horses were running and swimming from Assateague Island to another place called Chincoteague Island. One of the horses stopped in front of Grandma and it shook, and it shook, and it shook, and it shook, and it shook, and it shook, and it shook, and it shook, and it shook some more.

The horse made Grandma really wet from head to toe! "I should have stayed home. Old folks shouldn't be travelin'," said a very wet, very grumpy, Grandma.

Jasmine and Grandma finally arrived in New York City. As Jasmine and Grandma drove across the Williamsburg Bridge, the sun was shining brightly. She had always wanted to see what the East River looked like under the bridge, but every time she tried to look below a bright ray of light would shine in Grandma's eyes. *Sting. Sting. Sting. Sting.*

Grandma kept opening and closing her eyes so that she could see something. But each time she opened her eyes the sun bumped into them. Boing! Grandma said, "I should have stayed home. Old folks shouldn't be travelin'."

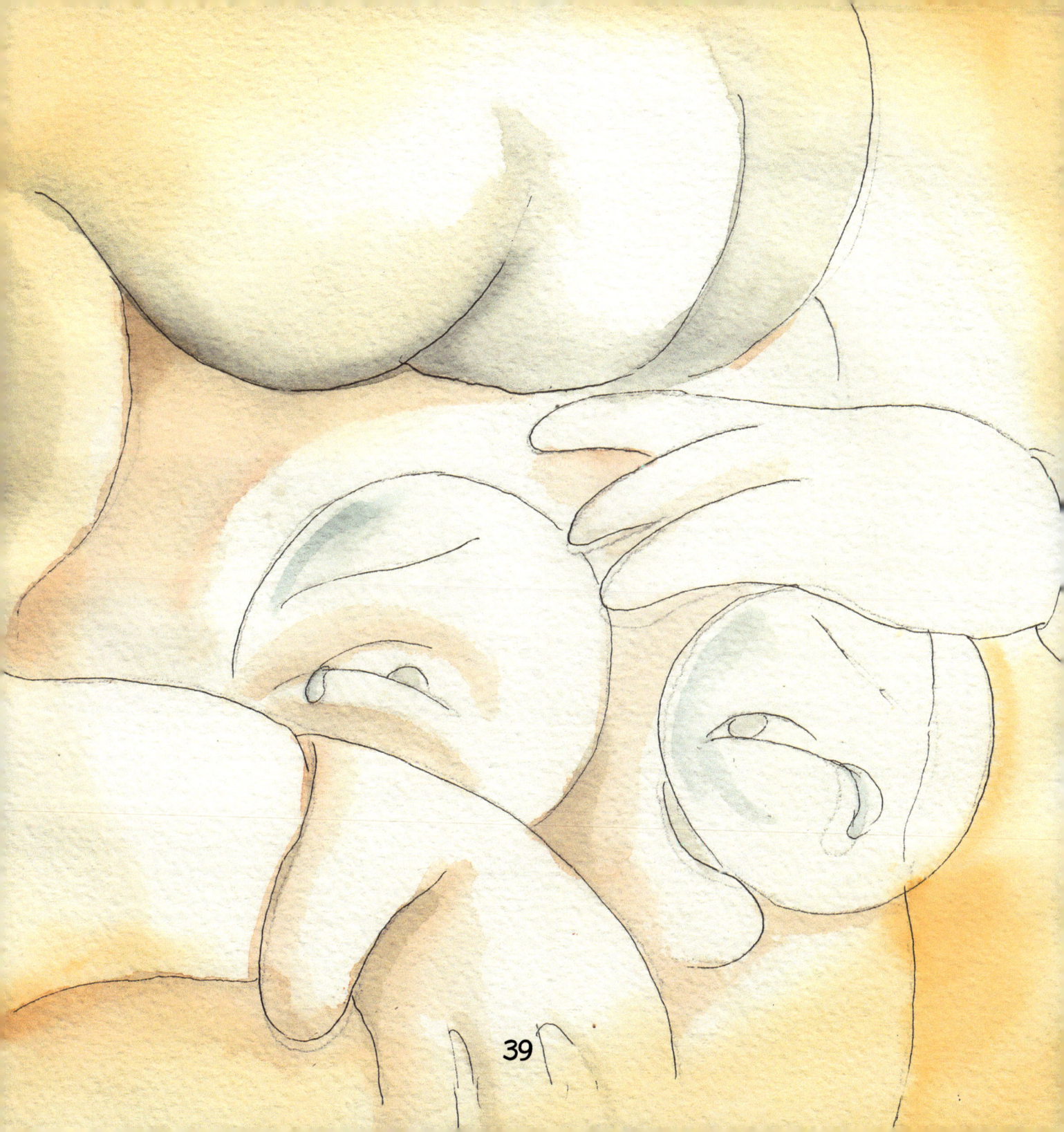

39

Jasmine and Grandma were a little tired after all of their driving, so they stopped on Graham Avenue in Brooklyn and went to a Puerto Rican restaurant. They had beans and rice and fried plantains. The food was delicious! But it was a hot day, so there were a lot of flies buzzing all over the place.

When Grandma opened her mouth to eat a bite of food, a big old fly flew right into her mouth. It flew so fast to the back of Grandma's throat that Grandma had to swallow it. Yuck!

With the yucky taste of the fly in her mouth, Grandma got so mad that she said, "I should have stayed home. Old folks shouldn't be travelin'."

With full stomachs, Jasmine and Grandma went to the Brooklyn Botanical Gardens. The gardens were so beautiful, especially the Japanese Garden that was full of natural stones, flowing water and lots of plants for frogs to sit on. Grandma walked across the bridge and over to the pagoda and sat down.

The sound of the water was so peaceful that Grandma soon fell asleep. When she woke up, a frog was sitting on her face looking right at her. Grandma screamed, "I should have stayed home. Old folks shouldn't be travelin'."

All rested up, Grandma and Jasmine continued on their journey. In order to reach Grandma's grandchildren, they had to take the Staten Island Ferry.

In the middle of the boat ride, while Grandma was trying on her life jacket, a seven year old on the upper deck thought it would be a good idea to go fishing. He tried to cast his fishing pole into the water, but the hook caught onto Grandma's life jacket. Thinking that he caught a big fish, the child started to pull Grandma up.

Not strong enough to pull Grandma up, the hook ripped through the life jacket and caught onto Grandma's wig instead, lifting it off her head and into the air. Grandma got so mad; she said "I should have stayed home. Old folks shouldn't be travelin'."

After taking a taxi from the Staten Island Ferry, Jasmine and Grandma finally reached the house of Grandma's grandchildren. It was a twenty story high brown building with many terraces and it was larger than any building Grandma had seen in her home town. She didn't like the tall buildings because she couldn't see the sun. However, it is where her grandchildren lived, so she and Jasmine went up to the elevator to the eighteenth floor apartment.

When the door was opened, Grandma found all one hundred of her grandchildren waiting in the apartment for her with smiles on their faces. One by one each grandchild gave Grandma a big hug. Grandma liked this! She liked it so much that she said, "I'm glad that I didn't stay home. Maybe Old folks should travel. Well, maybe just a little."

www.ingramcontent.com/pod-product-compliance
Lightning Source LLC
LaVergne TN
LVHW072119070426
835511LV00002B/22

9780996074100